MARIA

STADNICKA

The Unmoving

Broken Sleep Books
brokensleepbooks.com

Published 2018,
Broken Sleep Books:
Cornwall

brokensleepbooks.com

First Edition

Lay out your unrest.

Publisher/Editor: Aaron Kent
Editor: Charlie Baylis

Typeset in UK by Aaron Kent

Broken Sleep Books is committed to
a sustainable future for our planet,
and therefore uses print on
demand publication.

brokensleepbooks@gmail.com

ISBN-13: 978-1722286101
ISBN-10: 1722286105

'He made clothes for his children, dresses for his wife, suits for himself. But he kept it a secret. It was thought to be no work for a soldier.'
  - Alexander Solzhenitsyn

'So much guilt behind them and such beauty!'
  - Czeslaw Milosz

Contents

THE UNMOVING

Verbatim

We have silently waited for this moment
of crossing over
hand in hand
two worlds locked in a perfect house
in darkness, ready for guests.

The anonymous brick understands the material balance
between 'o' and other letters which
we have not yet brought forth.

A bridge builds itself
ahead of a thousand year journey.

Grand Vitesse

Most things depend on
a slowly deflating beach ball,

one town wired up to a dimmer switch
and someone is turning it out.

You could lay awake obsessing
about a blind woman
just met in the supermarket,
about the girl in Central America
travelling north on a sinking boat.

In clear daylight, the quartet
almost above the wave.

Nothing escapes the murmur,
all that was meant to follow somehow
slips through a tight net of thoughts.

A single bone rubs against bone
and only one key left.

Coming back to earth after a short season
in the chemical universe.
And what a let-down.

Cadence

A moon of salt unravels
the shadow between years,
unfolding a passage
grey chapter about mortality.

I hesitate
at the beginning of my fist fight.

I am snowing adult tears.

Pater Noster, I believe.
Now, slaughter my name.

Seeds

Nowhere else but here
the wounds of freedom have matured
among waiting vessels.

Exactly at this junction, there is
a number for everything.
The eyes follow the hypnotic replay of a horse race
losing sight of pieces falling across the shore.

This handful of random seeds,
two hundred and seventy-three souls.

Something sinister grows in the background.

An innocent opens the arch
to let a clutter of consonants out in the open.

The absence, with its comforts, jumps out
like a soundless gunshot.

Among people, to witness the whole procession and
to remain mountain.

Restitutio

I covered my face with black ink
rounded all my possessions up
set fire to everything.

My burning hand waved at
imaginary maps
disturbed the fish and the seed
with a silenced echo.

The gods hid in a poem
with a fresh loaf.

Just us now slicing away
to the end of my days.

Takeaway
for Aidan Semmens

Hello. I am a feature
on a CCTV camera, with
private resonance.

At the top floor, I
can barely sleep for the sound of gunfire.

I hear poetry when I pay for a pizza.

Hello, bullet. Welcome back to my flesh.
We are both refugees, I gather.

Urban Winter

At times, the metal sparks beneath roots. Knock.

The gap between things has grown,
it has become the present, the man's hostage.

Fluid traces of gunpowder drip on my place of safety.

A creature comes home to ask what solitude is...
take a dictionary, search, Alice...

In one space, I preserve this urban winter
among other forbidden emotions.

Only the presence of dust makes everything vibrant.

Dear Beckett, you came into being at the right moment.

So much I had to believe only to
get from one place to another.

Everyone likes a closer look at tragedy.

Atomic Day

I stop at a forgotten desk
in the intercity bus station
and write letters back to
a stone-temple

light a cigarette or a candle
they both smell carnal

the driver checks tickets
one passenger pushes in
through the cobwebbed rear mirror

to me, dear dictator, such an atomic day
looks more and more
like an open cathedral
everybody
can see me holding a timing grenade

I read again

swallow a handful of earth
for each word.

Thought 177

Seven o'clock. The streetlights are off.
Two children cross the Silk Road in high-visibility jackets.
The soldierly walk interrupts the sound of a bird.

The dead and the living unite in this perpetual defeat,
indifferent to our sleep-deprived reality.

Everybody has the same long list of alternatives,
they are only following orders.

Civil War

She opened the market early and people
queued to buy her flower baskets.
Her picture was politic.

Her essence divided the neighbourhood
to the point of a civil war.

At lunch time, she sat on a bench, neatly opposite South Bank
and watched the parade with a book on her lap.

When I saw her again, after years of absence,
one day in Montpellier Square,
she had lost her hair, had taken a vow of silence.

Death walked towards me, holding an empty paper bag.

Eyewitness 73

Back home from the cinema
I stumbled over a man in a pool of blood.
A bullet-hole in the back of his coat.
His book hanging from a lamp-post.

A night-bird stood over him.

An expectation to clear the area
shot through the blue hour.
Many tourists, working-suits, the bridge closed.
A few made it across.

One woman run off in a state of emergency.

A newspaper broke down in tears.

Movement

For almost a whole day I kept on moving forward
holding hands with an early summer heartbreak:
aluminium skies, closed high buildings, Cecilia Bartoli,
indefinite answers,
cut meadows, white hungry dogs,
unreachable glass bead.

At separate tables, the healthy and the sick.
The trees sat together knowing that life was actually
simple.

For far too long it felt I'd taken the wrong turn.
The long-dead drop whispered
that I should be ashamed of myself.

Migrant Bites. Day One.
to Elsie de Baron

We make noise and walk through the meadow
on high heels
fearful of mosquito bites
foreign English soil growing-growing an invisible
desert

'Come to mummy' I say arranging her cap,
'have a lollipop'.

A bruise on my back, map for water landscapes.

The wall keeps following me.

Traffic Jam
for Carl Henson

Where he went, against the perfect neon light,
he built a cube, a circle and one line
with both hands folded as if he'd prayed

the black-white memory of his mother
floated above cities long ruined

he believed in time, in mistakes –
the heroic stare of heavy hours

equally empty for everybody.

He sat in his bed like a tall ship
with the smell of reality in his mouth
ready to leave the port at any moment.

The Unmoving

I fell asleep by a window
the book slipped through my knees.

The world clean, in absolute isolation,
a time-capsule sent flying into space.

A missile woke me up half-dreaming
the outside watched
a man slowly walking between cars
on the high-speed motorway.

A few people passed by
out of nowhere
offered to sell me a dog.

The music absorbed what was left of Rana Plaza
the spring barked at young trees
another man took my place
born out of my faults.

The ground settled between reference points.

Germinal

I knew that a man died
being swept out to sea

at my breast an abstract image,
the meat I had waited for
pointing the finger at me.

One sunny day in the whole year
and, on arrival, all I could see was the hawk.

The chill in the ward slipped into my life
and became guilt.

Unavoidable present.

Graffiti

I imagined the return at the end of my sentence
on a street in Moscow
thinking the worst was already over.

I rushed at the gate
but something warned me.

The guards let me loose in a swamp.
What use was running to me?

I had carefully bathed,
tucked handkerchiefs in my pocket
where the children would search to find sweets.

I had no idea why everybody looked away.

The submission window for miracles closed
and I missed the deadline.

Street Corner

A chill sliced through the city
awoken stone rolled over the main road
as if that slippery thought
crossed my wrist.

Having to live with the small print for now
I watch the cars overtaking each other
almost planning an exit.

Some things avoid me.
A question leans against a wall
by the railway station.

Gloria mundi.

Afterthought

Each unavoidable thing has a squeal of its own
clean mirror placed at equal distance
between the beginning and the end of a day.

Each body spends time in the garden,
keeping the children still on long washing lines.

The afternoon explodes in small-smaller particles.
Shiny milk teeth block the emergency exit.

Unformed

It seems strange. The wait
leading to a place of execution

my embryo hanged by the neck until dead,
my direction leading to identical bus shelters.

Traffic signs in a maize.

The back alleyway hides a volatile crowd.
Blocked at both ends.

More push in through the barbed wire. Not an inch
of movement. Achtung!

Give me a handful of stones and watch
the staircase being built under constant attack.

Mandelstam

I thought I heard the door being unlocked
the one usually kept open to circumstance.
It happened. My older self just passing through.

I became a womb for grown-up houseplants,
hoped it would be water,
 it would be more,
 it would stay alive.

An eagle took off from a blank page.
Everything stayed buried in brimstone.

I said to him: 'Teach me to read Rublev's majestic blue,
everything written on my skin over so many years,
the irrelevance of blood-red victories.'

He gave way to a pilgrim fallen indoors,
a moth negotiating its destiny with each letter. Replied:

'Be happy, you are forgiven.'

For the first time, I
walked. Blind, absent.
I became tomorrow.

Acknowledgments

These poems were previously published in *Axon (Australia)*, *Dispatches Poetry Wars*, *Dissident Voice (US)*, *International Times*, *The Journal*, *Stride*, *Ink, Sweat & Tears*, *The Poets' Republic (UK)*, *Ofi Press Journal (Mexico)*.

A different version of Urban Winter, co-authored with Rupert Loydell, appeared in *TEXT (Australasian Association of Writing Programs)*.

Thanks to

Jane for twenty-nine hours, and not a bad word.

Rupert for four hundred and twelve emails, and not a single 'x'.

John for twenty black and white photographs.

Aaron and **Charlie** for building this room out of paper.

Mark for nine hundred and ninety miles travelled at night, and only for this book.

and

to **Ioan** who would have whistled.

LAY OUT YOUR UNREST

Printed in Great Britain
by Amazon